Time Management

How to Multitask, Improve Productivity and Stop Procrastination

Lance MacNeil

Table of Contents

Introduction

At one point in our life most of us have stopped for a moment or two, opened our eyes widely and just admired the person standing in front of us. How do some people do it? Where is the catch? And why is it always you that is struggling to stay in touch with the fast pace of your everyday routine? It's all about managing your time. Mastering this skill is essential for maximizing the outcome of your daily obligations and using your free time in an efficient way.

Following the guidelines offered in this book will help you successfully avoid the traps of a busy schedule and enable you to quickly, easily, and effectively develop your time management skills. Through understanding the notions of procrastination, multitasking and stress-free productivity, you will be offered the opportunity to alter your perception of time and, most importantly, set yourself free from a chaotic and unproductive schedule.

1: The Psychology of Time

Our perception of time is changing all the time. Whether it depends on the emotional state we are in at any particular moment or the activities we are involved in, we tend to perceive time differently. You have probably experienced the illusion of eternity, when sitting quietly in your dentist's waiting room for a whole five minutes. Similarly, sometimes time seems to fly, especially when we are enjoying ourselves; the night is never long enough, when you spend it with your friend who you haven't seen in years.

Why does this happen? Why does time sometimes seem so inconceivable, so paradoxical? Because that is exactly what time is. As such, it has the power to shape our behavior in the world that surrounds us and our lives in general.

The paradoxes of time

Time is one of the most intense influences on our day-to-day life. Not only does it affect our daily routine, our plans and schedule, it has an impact on our feelings and thoughts. Sometimes only time can cure a broken heart, especially when you lose someone who had a special place in your life. What about that embarrassing thing that you did way back when you were still in high school? So many years have passed that you probably don't even think about it anymore. However obvious it seems, most of us are totally unaware of the effect of the time on our life. This is the first paradox of time.

How we perceive time depends greatly on our personal experience. Waiting for your dentist to call your name wouldn't be so frightening if you wouldn't connect this to a past (probably painful) experience. This means that individual attitudes towards time are in fact a product of an individual experience. On the other side, time seems to be accepted as a social standard; 10 hours at work for me is the same as 10 hours at work for you. A century means the same for you as it does for him. Let's call this paradox number two.

The third paradox is a bit tricky. Specific attitudes toward time can be associated with various benefits. To be punctual is considered to be a quality that everybody should possess in today's fast-paced world.

Punctuality is accepted as a virtue and you are rewarded by society just because you are able to act accordingly. However, obeying social norms too much can also be a bad thing. Being rigid and not able to adapt quickly to changes in the schedule can hinder you in getting that promotion at work you always wanted or it can turn your personal life upside down.

Here lies the reason why time management is so important and at the same time it also represents the necessity for it. Ah, paradoxes.

Subjective experience of time

We all draw on memories from the past and plan our future based on our present experience of the world around us. How effectively we are able to do it and in what way we do it determines our life paths. Our perspective of time can influence everything from our success at work to our health and happiness. Understanding what time is and where we stand in its course is mostly learned in early childhood. Yes, probably you have inherited some behavioral patterns from your parents.

However this doesn't mean that you can change your point of view. If you think your personal time perspective hinders you in getting things done, you can by all means do something about it. The first step is to become acquainted with them and identify your own type:

The "Past-Negative" perspective

You tend to focus on negative personal experiences from your past and allow them to haunt you. This can make you feel bitter and sad more often that you would like to admit.

The "Past-Positive" perspective

You look at your past through the eyes of nostalgia. Staying close to your family therefore seems like the only reasonable behavior. Your relationships are happy; however taking risk is not what you are best at. This "safety first" attitude can hold you back in many fields.

The "Present-Hedonistic" perspective

Seeking pleasure in life and reluctance to postpone feeling good even for an hour makes you popular with your friends. However, you tend to have unhealthier lifestyle and take more risks.

The "Present-Fatalistic" perspective

You tend to feel trapped in the present instead of enjoying it. The sense of inability to influence what is going to happen in the future can lead to depression, anxiety and taking more risks than you should.

The "Future-Focused" perspective

You are goal-oriented and ambitious individual. However, while always trying to be an over-achiever, you can sometimes create stress for you and the people that surround you. Your relationships can suffer because of that.

Effective Usage of the Time Perspective

Believing that you are in control of the future and understanding that the past is, well, past, can empower you and give you a sense of control over your present actions. Finding the time perspective which will realize your psychological needs and your values is therefore more than important. Positive attitude towards what lies ahead and balance in general originate from making positive usage of your past and finding suitable ways to enjoy the present. After observing and understanding it, you start making plans for improvement and needed changes.

Let's presume that you are having problems with deadlines. Most of us do. It is really not that abnormal when you think about it. However, how you are going to deal with that is completely up to you. Missing a deadline is never easy and it always has some consequences. Meeting your boss the last time you missed one was not a walk in the park. Now, there are (at least) two possibilities for the future.

In the first possibility, you will hold on to the feelings of regret and embarrassment that you felt. Doing so will probably not help you to be more productive and efficient in your next project. The second option is to analyze the event and try to find room for improvement.

In time you will start to trust yourself and believe that you can actually do it in time. Believing that the future is not that bad can certainly increase the possibility that it will in fact be positive.

2: Time Management: The Flow Model

Sometimes, yet not often enough we find ourselves involved in an activity that we enjoy so much that time seems to fly by. Time becomes something completely irrelevant, redundant, and almost nonexistent. At that moment we completely focus our attention on what we are doing without even thinking about it. Everything around us – from the sound of ringing phones to the people passing falls beyond our comprehension. Yet the feeling of joyfulness is there somewhere deep inside us, keeping us energized.

Psychologists call this the "flow". When we are in the flow we tend to lose our sense of self and operate on our instincts alone. This allows us to completely devote to the task we are engaged in and enables us to be more productive. Reaching the state of flow can therefore make some task seem easier than they actually are, making us more efficient in what we do. Just imagine if everything you do in your life would appear easy or even trivial.

No more overthinking about how to solve a problem, no more worrying about the next task before you even complete the first. It would be like having a super power (as you always wanted). Well, it is maybe not that simple and straightforward but mastering this skill can still help you in managing your time.

The Flow Model

The model originates from the positive psychology niche from a few decades ago. Sounds fancy, right? But it's not that special. Positive psychology tends to use science to help us achieve a satisfactory life.

Bearing this in mind, we can say that the flow model tries to explain how emotional states, which human beings usually experience, can influence our perception of difficulty of a particular task.

On the other hand, the model predicts the emotional states we are most likely to experience when we try to complete a particular task. This greatly depends on how difficult this tasks seem to us and what we think about our ability to actually perform it.

The figure below will give you a bit more insight about this theory. If a task we are involved in is not challenging and doesn't require whole lot of skills, we are more likely to feel apathy towards it. If we are facing a challenging task without having the required skills we could start worrying about it which could result in the feeling of anxiety.

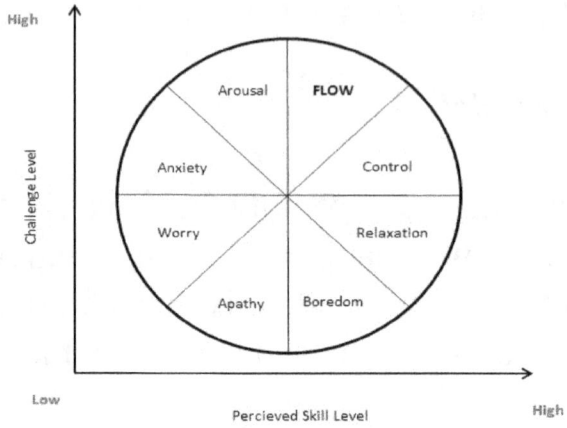

To be able to perform at our best and to find a balance we need a challenge that is interesting and can attract our attention, and an adequate set of skills to confidentially and successfully finish it. When these conditions are met we experience "flow".

When you learn how to reach it, you will become a part of the group of individuals who have mastered their art, business, hobby, or sport to a level so high that they make whatever they are doing appear easy.

The Components of Flow

Experiencing flow seems rather obvious now, when you know what it is. Roughly it can be divided into ten subcategories which, when combined, enable us to perform with the best possible efficiency rate, without wasting time or energy:

- Clearly understanding what we want to achieve

- Having the ability to concentrate for a long period of time

- Losing the feeling of consciousness of ourselves

- Realizing that time passes faster than usual

- Receiving immediate and direct feedback

- Experiencing a balance between the challenge and our skill levels

- Being in control of the situation

- Feeling of reward coming from being involved in the activity

- Not being aware of bodily needs

- Being completely engaged in the activity

In case you are starting to feel hungry or thirsty after a couple of hours of working, it doesn't necessarily mean that you are doing something wrong. It may simply be an indicator that you have been doing something right for so long, that your body needed an additional input of energy. The same goes for concentration; some people simply lack the ability to stay concentrated for a long time.

This doesn't automatically imply that they are unable to reach the state of flow. All of these experiences and factors don't necessarily have to be in place for the flow to happen. However a possibility exists that you might experience most of them when flow occurs.

The Conditions of Flow

Experiencing few or all of the components of flow is completely subjective. Some of us can experience all, for others a sense of personal control is enough. Whatever your case might be, there are three essential things that must be presents to enter the state of flow:

- First, you must have your ***Goals*** set: Goals add structure, motivation, and meaning to the activity you are involved in. It doesn't really matter what that activity is; you might be creating a presentation for a meeting or simply trying to get in shape by running every morning. You must be able to expect the final results and adapt your efforts and engagement in that particular activity accordingly.

- A good ***Balance*** between perceived challenge of the task and your perceived skills must be present. In case that one of these outweighs the other you may not achieve flow. If the activity is too easy, you will probably get bored. Occupying yourself with the coloring book and trying to stay inside the lines was maybe challenging when you were four, but now it would quickly get boring. Exaggeration? Probably, but the principle can be applied to whatever you might choose to do.

- Getting immediate and clear ***Feedback*** constitutes the third condition of flow. In order to make changes and improve your performance, you have to get in touch with what you are doing right and where there is still room for improvement. Feedback can come from others or it can originate from your awareness that you are (or not) making progress with the task.

Using the Model

In theory everybody knows how to cook a pot roast. All you need to do is to buy a 5-pound chuck roast, do something with it and enjoy the tasty and juicy meal. The same goes for the flow model. Understanding theoretical background of the model is one thing, but using it in a way that it will allow you to save time and be more effective in what you do is something completely different. But worry not. Simply bear in mind a few simple guidelines:

Setting the Goals

Goal setting was already established as a condition for flow. However, learning how to set effective goals can help you to achieve the focus you need. There are many way to set your goals. The creation of a daily to-do list is just a simple example of numerous approaches. The whole book could probably be written on this topic. Nonetheless, there are few things all the approaches are based on:

1) *Set positive goals*

Expressing goals in a positive, motivating way should be your objective here. This can make a difference for your attitude towards an assignment. "Try to do this successfully!" will give you the needed boost and motivation as in comparison to "Don't mess it up!" So, put in some effort and make the best list of goals that ever existed.

2) *Be precise*

Setting loose-end goals can give you some room to maneuver, which can surely make you feel good about yourself when the goal is not reached. However, to reach productivity your goals should be precise and accurate. Include dates, times, and amounts that will allow you to measure achievements. In this way, you will know exactly when the goal is reached and when you are prepared to move on to the next item on your list.

3) *Set priorities*

Some of us want to finish our training routine before we start to clean the apartment and some tend to have a power nap before committing to their afternoon tasks. It doesn't matter how you set your priorities as long as they allow you to stay within your goals. Another positive side of prioritizing is that it can help you to focus your attention to the most important goals, which can help you to avoid feeling overwhelmed by having too many of them.

4) *Write goals down*

Seeing something written on a paper, especially in your own hand writing can help you to remember why you even set a particular goal in the first place. Emotional memory is a powerful thing if you know how to use it.

5) *Keep operational goals small*

Tasks from a field we are not familiar with or simply do not like can appear impossible to finish. Breaking them down into a set of minor tasks usually overcomes this feeling. It is easier to have small, prioritized goals that you can easily reach.

6) *Set performance goals, not outcome goals*

Set goals over which you have as much control as possible. It can be devastating to set a personal goal and fail to reach it due to some external factor. Basing your goals on personal performance will allow you to keep control over your achievements and enable you to get satisfaction from them.

7) *Set realistic goals*

You will probably not be able to achieve world peace or develop a time machine in your life time. Realistic goals are the key here. Try to stay within the limits and set the goals you can achieve. If the goal is too broad and too difficult to achieve you also might not understand or appreciate the obstacles that you might encounter. This can lead to misconceptions of potential solutions of the problem.

Improving concentration

Not allowing yourself to be distracted by the trivial things happening around you is a skill. It is way too easy to check your email, or your Facebook feed every now and then, especially when you should be working really hard. Reaching the flow with these kinds of working habits is virtually impossible. You might consider using some strategies that could improve you concentration and allow you to stay focused and productive. Here, we provide a sample of a game which is usually used as an assessment in cognitive neuroscience to measure a part of working memory.

1) *n-back game*

Since it was introduce in the 1960s it became widely used for focus and attention training. As these components represent a major part of ability to concentrate, you can use the modified version for day-to-day concentration training.

First, you need to decide what kind of a stimulus you want to use. You can play around with words, colors or even sounds. After deciding, you will have to set a sequence of the stimuli you have selected. Your task from this point is to indicate the stimulus from *n*-steps earlier in the sequence, while still trying to memorize the newly presented stimulus.

The easiest way to do this is to make a note cards and practice verbally. For starters, below examples will suffice. Later, you can start modifying the rules or adding additional stimuli.

1-Back

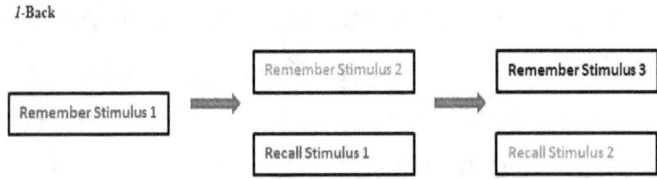

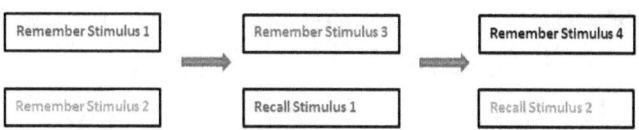

Building Self-Confidence

Skills are important, but if you don't have confidence in yourself there is a chance you won't be able to take full advantage of them. Lowering your self-confidence can sometimes happen in the blink of an eye; one wrong move or a silly comment and your ego can get hurt. Usually we are stronger than this; however, the chance to be affected by an inconsiderate remark remains. Building confidence is a completely different story.

The process involves in-depth analysis of your personality which usually leads to development of new attitudes towards different aspects of your life. However, what you can do easily is to perform a personal SWOT analysis. It will help you to stay focused on your strengths and allow you to better your weaknesses.

1) *Personal SWOT analysis*

A SWOT matrix is a framework meant for analyzing **Strengths** and **Weaknesses** as well as the **Opportunities** and **Threats** that you face. It is designed to help you focus on minimizing your weaknesses, focusing on your strengths, and take advantage of opportunities available for you.

The table below is design to guide you through the process.

Strengths	Weaknesses
What can you do?	What could you improve?
What might others see as your strengths?	What might other see as your weaknesses?
Which of your achievements are you most proud of?	What tasks do you usually avoid because of a lack of confidence?
Opportunities	**Threats**
What kind of opportunities do you usually seek in life?	What obstacles do you currently face in general?
Which trends/technologies/connecti ons could you take advantage of?	What is your competition doing?
Is there a way to turn your strengths into opportunities?	What threats do your weaknesses expose you to?

2) *Receiving Feedback*

Feedback is one of the most important elements of the flow. While appropriate feedback systems are important and you should make sure that they are properly used, keeping an open mind is even more important. Allow yourself and people around you to give you the information that might improve your performance. This applies to work situations as well as private ones. If your friends are complaining that you are always late, there must be something to it. Listen, consider, and adapt.

Making Work More Challenging

Adequate level of challenge can mean greater satisfaction when the job is complete. You don't need to go crazy about it; however, you can consider a job crafting strategy that will allow you to alternate your attitude towards even the seemingly most tedious jobs:

1) Decide what you want to change within a task? (*Can you make it more interesting, fun, or can you even combine it with another task?*)

2) Evaluate the potentials of this kind of change! (*Can you save some time doing it differently?*)

3) Act to put the change in place! (*Try to actually do it. Remember, goals are important*).

4) Observe your progress, adjust and continue (*Try to get the most out of it*).

All of the above techniques are designed to alternate your attitude towards time and adjust your basic behavior accordingly. It is the initial, most important step towards mastering the skills of time management and as such represents the basis for everything that follows in this book.

The following chapters are designed to make the best use of your newly developed attitude towards time. As mentioned above, reaching a particular mental state is one thing. Transforming it into observable results is something completely different. There are still numerous things that need to be addressed. One of them is definitely productivity.

3: Productivity - The Myth of Multitasking

Many people take great pride in being efficient multitaskers. Watching TV while having a meaningful conversation and obtaining the ability to do some work for tomorrow appear as something everyone tends to do. It allows us to join our tasks and errands into one, multidimensional cluster.

Doing it all at the same time now will allow us to take some rest later so we can focus our energy on do something else. This may just be true, but how effective is it really? How productive can we be if we are doing two or more things at the same time? The illusion of productivity exists but are we just disguising our pour attempts at one task by doing many of them at once?

Multitasking involves engaging in at least two tasks simultaneously. This can only be possible if at least one of those tasks is so well learned that we don't need to focus our mental effort to perform it. We should be able to do it automatically, like eating or walking.

Even more importantly, different tasks can involve the same brain mechanisms. As you might notice by yourself, focusing on the lyrics of a song while trying to read significantly lowers your ability to retain information about the topic covered in the book.

This happens because both tasks activate the brain's language center. Information from one interferes with the information obtained from other which significantly hinders your ability to pay attention to both. Just imagine talking to two people about two different topics at the same time.

On the other hand, listening to music doesn't affect your ability to drive a car. This is because listening to music activates different brain regions that have nothing to do with you motor skills. But is this really multitasking or does it simply mean that human cognition is a multidimensional thing?

Does multitasking even exist? Researches from the fields of cognitive science and psychology have discovered that our minds are not designed for heavy-duty multitasking. We simply don't have the mental capacity to effectively do it. Going into detail about this would turn this book into a neuroscience handbook. We won't do this. But the fact still remains that we are simply not wired to do it.

Serial tasking

At some point in our life we were all in the situation where we needed to do two things at the time - whether it was talking on the phone and listening to a radio show, or doing physical exercises and explaining to your friend how our weekend was.

Instead of "multitasking", a more accurate term to describe this would be "serial tasking". When subjected to many different tasks, we are not engaging in them simultaneously but rather shifting from one task to another in rapid succession. For example: you switch from a phone conversation to listening to a radio show and back again to your phone. This gives you the illusion that you are doing it at the same time when you are actually not.

But that's enough of this hair-splitting business for now. What is more interesting here is the effect this kind of task-solving has on our productivity.

Switching Costs

Switching between tasks takes a lot of energy. Frankly, it can be exhausting. Imagine yourself continuously running from one side of the room to the other in an attempt to be at both sides at once.

This mental juggling therefore claims some costs; costs that can lower the successful outcome of a job, task, or whatever you want to do. Even more importantly, these switching costs usually influence the time that you need to finish an assignment.

While serial tasking can appear as a faster solution to solve two or more problems, it can actually take more time than if each of those problems is addressed individually. Usually, switching costs are not that high but they can accumulate through the long periods of time. The longer the serial-tasking period is the longer are the switching costs.

Goal Shifting and Rule Activation

People tend to undergo two distinct phases when confronted to a situation which demands their full attention to be split to different fields. The first stage is called **Goal Shifting**. It is really simple: when doing two different things, we need to decide which one is more important to us. We have to ask ourselves a question and answer it. Something like this: "I want to do this now instead of that."

The second stage is **Rule Activation**. We are masters of adapting the rules to our needs. The same happens when we are deciding how we want to undertake a certain task.

At this stage, we tend to turn off the rules for *this* and turn them on for *that*. Example: there is a deadline for two reports. Both are important but you won't be able to finish them both in time. First, you need to decide what you want to do. You then go through the phase of goal shifting. When you decide which way you want to go, you probably still don't feel very confident that your decision was correct, so you start to bend the existing rules: "Ok, I'm going to finish the first report, because I have to, but the second one - that one can wait, it is not that important anyway."

Shifting between goals and activating the rules that suit you best is not considered harmful. It can actually be quite useful. It can help you to get the job done. The problem appears when, during this process, the switching costs are so large that they interfere with your productivity. In this case, your actions can become counterproductive and as such just draining energy from you without any visible results.

Choosing the strategy to boost the efficiency of multitasking

- *Avoidance*

The most effective attempt to increase your productivity is to stop multitasking, or better serial tasking. Try to focus on one task at a time and do your best at it. Many of the world's top athletes, businessmen, or programmers support this claim. The goal of those top performers is not simply to increase productivity and efficiency but to be the very best in their respective fields. Try adopting this strategy if you can and observe the results. For cases when this is just not possible, you can try to work with what you've got.

- *Training*

Whatever you might be doing - playing the piano or trying to learn how to juggle, repeating it over and over will increase your skills. At the same time, this will actually allow you to multitask more efficiently. When you master the piano to such a degree that you can play your favorite song without even thinking about it, a vivid discussion about the current political situation can take place while you are performing. Another step is to practice doing two things at the same time.

The same process will take place while doing so, but this time on a multi-dimensional level. Soon, you will be able to introduce watching TV into piano-discussion session.

You will have to decide for yourself what kind of activities the training should include. Regardless of the contents, the exercise could look something like this:

	Talking on the phone while driving can be dangerous
1	
2	
3	
4	

First Attempt:

1) Find a stopwatch and prepare to begin

2) Recopy the phrase "Talking on the phone while driving can be dangerous" in the third row. Immediately after that, move down a row and write down the numbers 1-43

3) After you have written down the last number, stop the timer and write down your total time.

Second Attempt:

1) Again, prepare the stopwatch. For best results, ask somebody to time you

2) Start with the letters of the phrase in the first row. For every letter, move down a row and write down its corresponding number

3) After the last number is written down, note your final time

4) Compare the final times of both attempts

5) Try to improve your multitasking time

Knowing when a task requires undivided attention

Switching focus between different things in a rapid succession can reduce your memory capacity. Think of your brain as a computer. Working with multiple programs and having numerous windows opened on your screen can slow down the operational capabilities of your machine. While it is pragmatic and it enables you to quickly jump between programs you need to complete your work; it can (and in most cases it does) result in a lock-up.

The same goes for your brain. When you are performing multiple tasks that require your undivided attention your brain can suffer from overload. Therefore try avoiding multitasking if the assignment requires your full attention. After the urgent part of the task is complete, you can return to your standard routine.

Using a tool to help you multitask

To avoid a (potential) mental overload and still be self-sufficient in what you do, you could seek some assistance offered by your environment.

Scientists call this phenomenon extended cognition. The simplest way to extend your thinking power is to take a piece of paper and write down some things.

But don't write down just everything. Accessing that information will require a special set of skills, not much different from the ones you are trying to mitigate. Write down things that you will use in a particular task the most.

If you are working with computers, have a list of most commonly used (and most easily forgettable) commands right beside your computer screen. If you are working in export department, some telephone numbers will definitely come in handy. Be creative and extend your cognition to your working space.

Allow your mind to reboot

Focusing your attention on a single task can help your mind to reboot. Our brain uses more energy than any part of the body. This capacity can be useful but it can also backfire. As computer needs a reboot every now and then, to be reminded who is the boss in that relationship, so does your brain.

Rest is one of the key components of increasing productivity. It may not sound as much, especially if you imagine yourself staring out the window for 15 minutes, but it may help in consolidating the information learned and making room for new things.

Every two to three hours you should take a 15-20 minutes break. You can also go for some fresh air and even for a walk if you have the option to do so. This will also increase your blood circulation and provide your brain with fresh supplies of oxygen and nutrition.

Taking a brain break

When you start to feel that your attention is drifting away, take a minute or two to relax. Even that short period of time should be enough to clear your mind for a while. Simple conversation with your co-worker can also do the trick.

The effect will last you for some time, at least until the time of your next walk or coffee break. And don't worry; most of the employers are aware of the effect of this kind of behavior on productivity. If you don't overdo it, they probably won't mind.

4: Stress-free Productivity

Preparing your schedule while having optimal productivity in mind all the time can be a difficult task. Worrying about increasing efficiency and how to get everything done in time can work on the short term; however, there is a possibility that you will not stay committed to the method. And it is normal; people sometimes need a break from all this order.

But then after a while you start thinking: why did I put so much time and effort in this? There must have been a reason. And you decide to continue with it. You prepare a plan from which you expect the maximum results: increased productivity and an additional hour a day, just for yourself.

After the first day everything seems fine. The second day, your boss announces that you will have to work overtime this week, the same week that your daughter has a piano recital, which you will have to miss. All that effort disappears in a split second.

Not reaching the goals can bring additional stress in your life. In addition, all time management tricks were useless because of the unpredictable change in your schedule. Setting priorities for example don't do the trick anymore when you are physically unable to perform the task.

Few things can help you to overcome this. The methods for personal productivity enhancement and reduction of the stress caused by information overload will help you to stay prepared.

Collect Information

Your first step will have to include gathering information from the environment. Collecting every piece of information that catches your attention is crucial in this step.

Note down everything that is potentially relevant to your activities, whatever its subjects, degree or urgency, and importance might be. This will most likely include phone calls, emails, newspaper articles, suggestions from your coworkers, memories, and personal ideas.

Use one of the tools of extended cognition to collect all of this information. Notebook or electronic organizer will do the trick here. We will call this your *In-basket*.

However, collecting is just the first part of this phase. You will have to select what is of value for you by emptying the **In-basket** regularly. Deciding what to do with the gathered information will give you control over the collected materials. To be really efficien,t you will have to process and organize the items one by one.

Process and Organize

Being organized makes things easier in general. Imagine if you have to search for your socks at random places in your house every morning. Keeping them in a designated drawer makes it easier to find them and saves you a lot of time and frustration.

The same goes with your tasks, plans, goals, and to-dos. After emptying your **In-basket,** you will need to process the remaining information and decide what to do with it. The simplest and still efficient way is to combine them into categories. They should be based on the lowest common denominator; either time, location, or the priority level.

These categories will represent all of your **Applicative files** that will enable you to increase your efficiency and productivity. Not only that, they are designed for you to plan your future actions in the least stressful way.

They could look something like this:

Action List:
- Buy present for wife
- Call John and ask about the project details

Project Plan: Vacation
- Make reservation at the hotel
- Book the plane tickets
- Get insurance

Calendar:
- March 23: Wedding anniversary
- April 2: Flying to France

Waiting for:
- The currency

Maybe:
- Read The Count of Monte Cristo

References:
- Booking conformation number: 659sd5

Review

As in most of the projects, the reviewing phase is crucial. It will help you to stay in touch and improve in your daily routine, and better manage your weekly tasks.

The daily review must include your *Calendar*, with emphasis on the most important things you have to do on a particular day. The second part of it is reviewing the *Action list*, what you should do as soon as possible.

The weekly review should be an in-depth analysis of your Applicative files: ***In-basket, Calendar, Action list, Projects, Project plan, Waiting for, and Maybe.*** It is especially important to get an overview of what you need to do in the coming time period. Again, this will give you the feeling of control. This control, in addition, result in keeping all of your files up-to-date. This will include even the most tedious and seemingly unimportant work, such as cleaning out your email or your desk.

This kind of review is also important in order to develop and maintain trust in your new system. Feelings of clarity and purpose will accompany this action. Regular attempts to organize your files will also help you in unpredicted events. Changing circumstances can quickly ruin your long-term plan if you don't adjust your daily and weekly schedule.

Perform

At some point your will find all your lists up-to-date. What about now? How should you decide what to do first? There are four criteria that you should take in consideration.

Context

You probably can't do the same things when you are sitting at your desk as when you are walking in the park. The environmental context limits your choices and most probably defines your behavior. In the case that your Action list is long, it is advised to organize it by the context (home, office, outside). This will enable you to cluster the actions that can be performed in the same context.

Time availability

Time is always an issue. However don't push yourself. This won't help anybody. Fit the duration of your actions to the amount you actually have available.

Energy availability

The same thing goes for your energy levels. Sometimes you have to accept that you are tired and in need of a nap. Doing things by force could result in a low quality performance. Chances are that you will have to repeat the task which can set you back in your time and energy.

Priority

Regarding the context, as well as your time and energy, you will have to decide which things should be done first. The "Threefold model" for evaluating daily work can help you decide:

Do work as it appears	Do predefined work	Define your work
• Go with the flow • Solve tasks as they appear • Don't allow tasks to pile up	• Systematically go through your Action list • Set priorities • If your list is empty define your work	• Similar to reviewing phase • clear your mind • Update your system

Your plan is set, your Applicative files are organized, even prioritizing doesn't seem a mystery anymore. The best thing now should be to start using these skills. However, your friend has a party tonight, and making this plan really precise would take a lot of energy and focus. Maybe it is better to do it tomorrow, when you actually have the will power to do it. Doing it today just wouldn't make sense.

This is where most of our time-management efforts start to collapse. Why are we so inclined to postpone our duties? Are we all just lazy or is there something more to it?

5: Postponing Your Duties

The simplest definition of procrastination includes putting off things that you should be focusing on right now. Usually this happens when we are doing something that is more enjoyable. There is always something good on TV when you should be writing your report. The day seems sunnier when you are stuck inside cleaning out your garage. Even the most annoying house work becomes interesting when you are forced to prepare for tomorrow's meeting.

Psychologist call this a time-gap between intended and actual. It sounds fancy, but at its core it simply means what everyone does from time to time: postponing the duties. Regarding this definition, it means that there is a large, measurable time period between when we want to do a job and when we have the will power and energy to actually do it.

Postponing duties doesn't necessarily mean that we are procrastinating. Sometimes there is a question of priorities. Your report can wait if you need to fix the water heater before it floods your house. You also won't leave your kids waiting at school for too long just because you should prepare for that meeting. Some things are just more important than others and you need to attend to them first.

Feeling particularly tired and taking a short nap before working around the house also doesn't necessarily constitute procrastinating behavior. If this is merely an occasional event and if it usually doesn't take too long you should definitely take a break from everything. Power naps can be beneficial as they allow your brain to reboot and your body to recover from a long working day.

Procrastinating behavior is commonly connected to making up excuses for even the simplest tasks. Perhaps you are in some sort of pain or the task is just impossible to perform; everything comes in handy when you really don't feel like doing something. That strange feeling that we feel in our stomach even when we think about doing it, is usually enough to convince ourselves that it can wait for a while.

Some tasks can wait, others simply can't. Although most of the time we are still able to do them in time, our behavior usually creates a stressful environment for us and people around us, our sleep cycle is interrupted and we are just generally tired and annoyed by our decision to wait for the last minute. The strangest thing is that in most cases this behavior is repetitive. We tend to repeat our decisions and our mistakes. Why do we tend to do this?

Common causes of procrastination

The reasons for procrastination can be found in the nature of the task but you are also responsible for it yourself. While they can be well blended together, it is important to understand which of the two is relevant in a given situation. This way you will be able to select your approach for changing your behavior and overcoming this habit.

Inconvenience

Often we find ourselves outside of our comfort zone. The reality doesn't fit our expectations, we feel insecure and small and we have this feeling that we just don't belong there. However, sometimes we are just acting in accordance with our preferences and find a particular job unpleasant, boring and redundant. In this case, we are preparing to do whatever is necessary to avoid it. We are searching for excuses and postponing the task for as long as possible.

When you look at it from this perspective you will see that most jobs have their unpleasant aspects. The best way to deal with this is to get them over and done quickly. Shift to your mental happy place and try to leave it behind as soon as possible. This way you will be able to focus on more enjoyable duties.

Disorganization

Another cause for procrastination is also of a personal nature. People who are organized, manage to overcome procrastination. Their to-do's and Action lists enable them to recognize how important a particular task really is. This way they recognize when it is due. Being organized also means knowing how long performing a task will take and therefore, when it should be addressed.

You can start with breaking the work down into small manageable steps. It is not much, but it will help you to understand the importance of your duties and how you should address them. Work within the notion of stress-free productivity to become organized in the long run.

Doubt

Even extremely developed organizational skills are not an assurance that you won't fall in the traps of procrastination. You can still feel overwhelmed by a particular task. Doubting that you possess the skills to produce satisfactory results can delay your decision to actually do what you need to do.

Seeking tasks that you know are in you comfort zone is quite common from this perspective.

The big task, unfortunately, will not just disappear. Sooner or later you will have to address it. Sometimes there is no other way than simply doing it. Ask yourself what you have to lose if you don't perform as expected. Nonetheless, we are just people, always in the process of learning.

Perfectionism

People who incline towards perfectionism are also likely to be perfectionists in procrastinating. They often postpone their duties as they want to perfect their skills which will enable them to achieve top-notch results. Doing it half way through is just not their way. It's everything or nothing.

While this can be helpful in some skill-intensive tasks, it can also mean that, if you have found yourself in this description, work will start to pile up. However, if you can manage to stay on track and still be efficient and productive, there is no need to start changing it now. But only if this is the case.

Lack of decision-making skills

Sometimes you have to be assertive and know what is best for you. If you are unable to make a decision when a situation urgently demands it, you are more likely to postpone taking action. Being afraid of taking actions that will lead to possible mistakes can result in putting things off as long as possible.

Situations can sometimes be complicated and confusing. However, you are here to take care of yourself. If nothing else, your Applicative files can help you to get the bigger picture of the situation and to make a decision accordingly.

6: Defense Mechanisms of Procrastinators

Being exposed to potentially harmful impulses coming from the environment or from our own inclinations is part of life. However, people, as amazing as we are, have the ability to cope with this kind of situation. This techniques helps us to reduce anxiety that can result from being confronted with something outside our comport zone.

Defense mechanisms, as we call them can take various different forms and may result in healthy or even unhealthy behavior, depending on the frequency of their use.

Procrastination itself could be placed in this category. It has all the quality of a defense mechanism; it allows us to cope with something that we don't feel comfortable doing and it can result in unhealthy behavior that robs us of our energy and efficiency.

However, as procrastination can become a habit that can cause us to feel anxious, most procrastinators have developed strategies to cope with it. Individual coping responses to procrastination usually serve the purpose of avoidance and emotional alienation rather than resolving this issue.

Emotional defense mechanisms are especially interesting. They are designed to reduce stress associated with putting off personal goals and provide pleasure in doing so. Most of the "highly-skilled" procrastinators use the following techniques:

Avoidance

Temporary retreating from a difficult situation is usually just another way of protecting ourselves from negative feeling that might arise from our perceived inability to perform well. Watching TV when we should work is a perfect example of this defense mechanism. However, putting off our task usually just makes the situation worse and as avoidance continues, it usually produces more anxiety which (sometimes) calls for using additional coping strategies.

Distraction

If avoidance isn't possible for any reason, distraction might come in handy. By engaging ourselves in different behaviors or actions we, at least for a while, forget about the task we need to attend. Browsing through random Facebook profiles seems a perfect solution to distract ourselves from writing, reading, or whatever we should be doing.

Trivialization

Trivializing tasks for which you would swear that they are the most important things in your life just a few days ago is a common strategy to justify our actions. That meeting that we should be prepared for is actually not as important as we claimed it was before.

Why bother to stress out if we simply don't have time for it? This kind of self-persuading can help us to feel better for a while but it won't make the task disappear. In addition, the consequences of trivialization can be long-lasting and serious.

Humor

It's actually funny how lazy we are. Let's just laugh it off and it is going to be fine. When we laugh, endorphins that reduce stress are released in our brain. This makes us feel happier and more relaxed, which can be a good thing for completing our duties. But we have to realize that while

laughter may be the best medicine, it isn't
necessarily very effective in producing work-
related results.

Denial

Denying procrastination is another defense
mechanism. We tend to convince ourselves that our
behavior doesn't actually constitute as
procrastination, but as something else. Being tired
is a perfect example of that. It might as well be
that we are tired when we should work, but it has to
come down to rationalization: are we really so
exhausted that we can't do the dishes tonight, or are
we just trying to avoid this unpleasant task?

Laziness

Laziness is a bit tricky. We can be regarded as lazy
because we tend to postpone our duties. On the
other hand, we could procrastinate because we are
lazy by nature. Whatever the truth is, being lazy is
usually just a way of avoiding the work that is
waiting to be done.

Valorization

Picture this: when we should be focusing on a task
from our Action list, we engage in a different

activity, let's say cooking. After completion, we are immensely proud of our achievement and feeling joyous that we skipped our duties for it. This is called valorization. Within this defense mechanism, we tend to feel excess satisfaction in what we achieve while we should have been doing something else.

In most cases, our defense mechanisms are not so clear. They are blended together into a productivity-proof cluster. However, you might notice that in a particular situation, one or two are stands out in the crowd. By addressing them and analyzing your behavior, it will be easier to understand and overcome the reasons for procrastination.

In the case that your laziness amuses you, you might have to consider why this is the case. Maybe the fact is that you really are lazy. But most probably, there is something more to it. You might want to address this issue and continue sticking to your Action list.

7: Procrastination Equation

Different people have different reasons for procrastinating. We also use different mechanisms to better cope with it. However, there are few common grounds for every procrastination related behavior.

- First, there is **Expectancy**. This notion applies to your expectation to reach your personal goals. Sometimes we tend to underestimate a particular task and believe that finishing it should be easy. If our understanding of it turns out to be false, we can develop resistance for it. When facing similar task in the future, our emotional memory can kick in and we start to believe that we can't handle the task anymore. Expecting failure can result in emergence of additional defense mechanisms which can lead to procrastinating behavior.

- *Value* can be regarded as the second component of procrastination. The value that a particular goal has for us is of great importance if we want to actually reach it. We found a particular task of low value for our personal needs, a great chance exists that we will try to avoid it by all means. Not even proven facts of a task's general importance for our well-being can force us to like something that we simply don't like.

- ***Impulsiveness*** is in general the biggest factor in procrastination. It is a part of a broader component of procrastination – time. When we are impulsive we tend to forget to follow our action plan and do what seems the most reasonable in the given moment. As time passes, we are more likely to forget about the task that we should focus on. The rewards of it completion starts to fade away and we, once again, start to use different defense mechanism and convince ourselves that it is actually not that important.

- The fact that some of our goals can be far away in the future can lead to a *Delay* in our decision to address them properly. This component, as the previous one, is also connected with rewards that we receive from our actions. The longer the delay of a particular task, the less motivated we become to do it. The problem here is also that we usually miscalculate the time of the potential start of the task. It may appear really distant, somewhere in the future, when in fact it is closer than we perceive it.

All of these components are very much interlinked and also connected to every other aspect of time management. It is impossible to say that impulsiveness is the core reason for procrastination without connecting it to the delay-award effect. And we can't talk about this without understanding the psychology of time perception.

The procrastination equation, while based on the four factors found in any kind of procrastination, therefore includes all of the factors described in this book. It takes all those notions to explain why we sometimes lack the motivation to do something that we so obviously should.

$$Motivation = \frac{Expectancy \times Value}{Impulsiveness \times Delay}$$

Procrastination for this perspective is defined as the product of expectancy and value, divided by the product of impulsiveness and delay.

But this can appear rather abstract. To understand how this equation works we have to put in in action. The best way to do it is to examine different types of procrastination and to try resolving them.

Low Expectancy

Imagine you are attending a seminar on time management. You read all the material; you arranged your to-do lists; and you paid attention to all the techniques mentioned by the lecturer. However, after few days you notice that not much has changed. People are still waiting for you, you still feel stressed and under the impression that your life is falling apart. Soon you decide that these actions are just not worth taking, turn on the TV and enjoy the rest of the day.

Your expectancy in this scenario was low. After no results were visible after a few days, you started to believe that nothing is ever going to work for you. You have started to expect only failure. Results from studies on procrastination show that low expectancy plays a great role in procrastinating behavior. Doubting your own abilities lowers your motivation to perform the task. You have learned to feel helpless based on your previous results.

Low Value

Now imagine that you have to write a report for your boss. The topic, while still a part of your work, is so boring that you simply can't sit down and start writing. When you finally do, after a whole 10 minutes of work, you decide to take a short break. Within this short break, you call your friend and a beer suddenly seems like a perfect idea. You finally start working when you return home late at night. While you still manage to do it in time, the quality of the report is now not as high as it could be.

The problem in this case is that the task has a very low value for you. Because of that you decide to put it off for as long as possible. It is easy to do this when you don't like something. Beer with a friend is easy, but working on something you find boring requires motivation. Due to low value, the motivation level is not high enough to convince you to start being productive.

Impulsiveness

There is a possibility that this has already happen to you. You started to plan you holidays abroad. The plane ticket was booked; you have exchanged your money and already started packing. You remembered that you still have to book your hotel room but in this chaotic situation, some things were just more important. When it was almost time to depart, you remembered that you forgot to do it. You made a last-minute reservation but when you arrived to your destination, the room was not what you expected.

While you knew you should have made the reservation in advance, some things were simply more important at the time. It would be easy to do it but you got distracted by more urgent or more interesting things. When you finally did it, it was almost too late.

Studies have shown that an event's impact on our decision decreases the farther away in the future it is. We tend to give priority to the awards that our goals can bring us now and are less motivated by the potential awards in the future. It is actually quite obvious. It is much more satisfying to get an ice cream when you actually want it than one week from that moment.

Beating Procrastination

Procrastination is a complex phenomenon which involves numerous psychological traits. We covered some of them, and some of them will be left for some other time. But enough with the theory, you have to start working on beating it.

Once you understand the procrastination equation, the possible strategies become quite obvious. While there is not much you can do about the delay effect of the reward, you may focus on the remaining components in which you do have more control. In order to beat procrastination you will, therefore, have to increase your expectancy of a positive outcome, take care of impulsiveness and increase the perceived value of the task.

Increasing Value

It can be difficult to stay motivated about something when it doesn't have much value to us. The good thing about value however, is that is somewhat relative. This means that we can modify our attitude and behavior in order to perceive the value of a task as higher.

Meaning

You can start by giving meaning to a particular task. You can connect it to something you care about or simply like. If you like singing you can sing while doing the dishes. This way you will start to connect this unpleasant task to something you enjoy doing.

The least that you can do is to connect the task to something you want through a chain: If you write a good report for your job now you might get a promotion later which will allow you to save more money and eventually you will be able to buy that sports car you really want.

Energy

Tasks appear much harder when you are tired. You might want to do the most demanding tasks when you feel most alert. This will make the task look easier even when you don't like it that much.

There are few things you can do to preserve your energy:

Exercise - Drink lots of water - Take power naps Listen to music to improve your mood - Take care of your diet

Rewards

You can increase the value of the task by rewarding yourself after successfully completing it. In the long run, this will help you to connect the task with something good that might follow. Arranging a reward system is completely up to you. Decide what you consider to be an adequate prize for you work and stick to it.

Taking Care of Impulsiveness

Taking care of impulsive behavior is equally important as increasing the value of your task. Here are two strategies that can help you with this.

- ### Committing now

Pure willpower is not always enough to produce results. The will easily disappear if you don't commit to the actual act of doing. Planning ahead can help you with this. If you know you can easily get distracted, try to address the issue in advance, when it still doesn't appear as urgent.

Another method you can use for committing now is to "throw away the keys". Close off tempting alternatives and focus your attention on what is important. Watching TV is a perfect example. Most people are more productive when they decide not to turn it on when they should be working.

You can also try applying the positive punishment technique. By exposing yourself to a mild punishment every time you don't reach your goal, you will quickly program your behavior and try to avoid these consequences. Not going for a beer in the evening is a perfect example of such a punishment.

- ▪ *Setting goals*

Goals are very important. Without a proper set of goals, you basically just wonder through life not knowing when you reach your destination. Apply the **SMART** approach to your goals, when thinking about what you want to achieve. Your goals should be:

- Specific
- Measurable
- Attainable
- Realistic
- Timely

Increasing Expectancy of Success

If you believe that you can't do something, chances are you are right. Attitude is everything from this perspective. If you think you can't succeed, you will have little motivation to do the thing you need to do. The most obvious advice would be to stay positive and believe in yourself. But how can you acquire this attitude? We have already covered this topic to some extent but here we provide some additional aspects of the topic, which will allow you to work on your positive attitude in general

The spiral effect

Successful performance can make you feel better and more optimistic about similar tasks in the future. You can set yourself a series of small challenges that are easy to solve. This will boost your ego and make you feel that you can do anything. Just be careful that the challenge is in accordance with your perceived skill level (remember: the flow!). After a while you can start mixing in tasks you are not sure about. You will notice the spill-over effect of the positive boost from the success spiral. It will enable you to develop a new, positive perspective on your ability to perform.

Creative Visualization

You can also try to imagine what you want to achieve and how to do it. Try to picture how good it will feel when you finish the report for your boss and what effects this could have on your future career. Research has shown that this method can substantially increase motivation for performing difficult tasks.

Another option is to imagine what will happen if you avoid doing the task you should be doing. Mental contrasting can have the same effect as creative visualization. It is up to you to decide which method you want to use. Some people likes carrots, others need the stick.

8: The Art of Time-Management

We have covered the theory and some practical advice on how to manage your time and be more efficient in general. Understanding this is necessary but not sufficient to actually manage your time properly. Dreaming is something, but transforming those dreams into reality is, in most cases, something completely different.

There are many ways of applying this knowledge of time management into real-life situations. You could start with examining your time perspective and adapt your behavior in a way that will allow you to be the most productive. You could initially focus on reaching the flow and allow everything else to follow your new attitude towards problem solving. Again, you should first start with increasing your multitasking skills.

At some point, if you want to master your time successfully, you will need to apply every aspect of it to your daily routine. This way of thinking should become your habit which should be incorporated in every single moment of your life.

Time management is not just a theory; it is a way of life. It is similar to becoming a professional athlete. Limiting your efforts to a single day of the week will bring you nowhere. It takes constant struggle and adaption to become really good.

It is possible to lose the motivation in the process, but with correct set of goals, you will continue until you achieve the unachievable. And as with sports (or any other thing), you have to start at the beginning.

Starting small: Daily strategies

Each and every one of us has a different way of life and hence a different daily routine. This is why it is difficult to propose an effective daily routine that will allow you to make better use of your time. You will have to think about your time-wasters yourself and make appropriate changes.

However, creating your Applicative files (including Action list, Project plan and a Calendar of your duties) should be one of your priorities. They will allow you to plan your day ahead and allow for a smooth transition between days and weeks.

There are a few things that you might miss on your list if you aren't careful. Addressing them in time will allow you to root them in your behavior and allow you to develop a better, healthier perspective on time management from the beginning. Small actions can have a great effect on your future; you just have to know how to address them.

Before work

1) Start creative work early

When you are still a bit sleepy, your mind works in a different way. You are more open to new ways of thinking and new ideas. Use this state to be creative. Imagine what you can do in the course of the day. It doesn't matter if it is reachable; the point is to exercise your mind. This will allow you to be better at problem solving later in the day.

2) Use little windows of time

Use the free time when you are waiting for your eggs to be boiled (or whatever your favorite breakfast might be) to do something productive. Standing in the kitchen and waiting will not force the eggs to be cooked sooner. Make this time count, whatever you decide to do.

3) Combine activities

We discussed that multitasking can be contra-productive. But there are exceptions. If you have a habit of reading the news every morning, do it while having breakfast. This is also beneficial for your digestion as researchers have shown that reading lowers the speed of eating, allowing your body to get more nutrition from it. In this case, combining activities is a positive thing.

In the office

1) *Plan for slightly less time for working*

Allow yourself a break after you finish a particular task. If your schedule is tight, plan in advance and include the break in you working time. This will give you a bit less time to work but the potential break will serve as a motivational reward. In case you don't finish, you can still use the break-time to do so and keep your schedule intact.

2) *Group related tasks*

If things can be combined they should be. There is no need to have one meeting now, and another one later if all the parties have time to have it in the morning.

3) *Return calls and check e-mails at a fixed time*

Set a specific time to return you calls and emails and try not to do it during your peak energy times (use those to do more productive things. This will make your working day less stressful.

4) *Learn to say no*

Sometimes it is just necessary. If you are overwhelmed with duties, just say no to new ones. It makes no sense to stress yourself about something you know in advance you can't finish in time. This should in fact be applied to all aspects of your day.

5) *Delegate your tasks*

It is good to be self-sufficient but sometimes other people can help you. If you have a busy schedule some aid from your co-worker can be invaluable.

Before sleep

1) *Schedule your typical time-wasters*

Try scheduling a specific time for watching TV or browsing the internet. These soothing activities can be beneficial for your productivity only if they are confined. Having your TV on when you have to focus on some other work can have a negative effect.

2) *Pretend the deadline is tomorrow*

It doesn't matter if the deadline is not until next week. Try to cope with your defense mechanism and pretend that it is tomorrow. You will see how much effect it can have on your willingness to actually do the task in question.

3) *Review your work from the previous day*

Feedback is important. It will allow you to learn from your actions and find room for improvement as well as understanding your progress. For a smooth transition between days, do a quick review of your work from the previous day. Writing it down will allow you to clear your mind and allow for a smooth transition to the next day.

Conclusion

There is no reason to beat yourself down if you are unsuccessful in managing your time. In today's fast-paced society, most people find themselves caught in situations that they can't control anymore. Stress has become a socially acceptable mental condition and work overload is a prerequisite for it.

Therefore, managing time not a simple walk in the park. A lot of effort and commitment is required in order to keep up with your busy schedule. And life is not just about work and tasks. We still have to find some time for ourselves, our family, and enjoy some fun time with our friends.

Just because it is difficult doesn't mean that it is impossible. You now have the knowledge of what is priority in order to be better with managing your time. You understand what actions you need to take in order to beat procrastination and to increase your productivity. The combination of the described approaches can serve as a good foundation for changing your habits and improving particular aspects of your life.

Some effort will still be required to achieve the full potential of effective time management. It may take some time to make the necessary changes. This is why you should just go for it and start doing it. There is nothing to lose and a whole lot to gain.

www.ingramcontent.com/pod-product-compliance
Lightning Source LLC
Chambersburg PA
CBHW070848180526
45168CB00002B/1001